RACHEL CAMILLA

How To Stop Overthinking Over An Abusive Husband

Contents

Introduction

In the intricate web of abusive relationships, the insidious companion known as overthinking weaves its way into the minds of victims, perpetuating a cycle of mental distress. This ebook delves into the complexities of overthinking, unraveling its threads as they intertwine with the dynamics of an abusive husband. As we embark on this exploration, it becomes evident that overthinking is not merely a casual contemplation but a relentless force that exacerbates the hardships faced by those ensnared in the clutches of abuse.

The impact of overthinking within the context of abusive relationships is profound and far-reaching. It serves as a silent accomplice, amplifying the emotional toll inflicted by an abusive partner. This ebook scrutinizes the detrimental consequences, shedding light on how overthinking intensifies feelings of fear, anxiety, and self-doubt. By understanding the intricacies of this mental process, we aim to dismantle the barriers it erects, ultimately fostering an environment conducive to healing and recovery.

Recognizing the symbiotic relationship between overthinking and mental health, this book "How To Stop Overthinking Over An Abusive Husband" emphasizes the imperative nature of addressing these intertwined issues. Mental health is a delicate tapestry, easily frayed by the incessant worries and self-criticisms that overthinking perpetuates. Through a comprehensive exploration of coping mechanisms, psychological insights, and empowerment strategies, we navigate a path towards reclaiming mental well-being.

Yet, woven into the narrative is an unwavering commitment to empowerment. The storyline takes a deliberate turn towards fostering strength and resilience. "How to Stop Overthinking Over an Abusive Husband" is not a mere examination of the problem; rather, it serves as a roadmap, guiding readers towards breaking free from the shackles of overthinking and nurturing hope for a future liberated from abusive relationships.

As we traverse the pages of subsequent chapters, each section becomes a crucial stepping stone, equipping readers with knowledge, strategies, and support to navigate the challenging terrain of abusive relationships while concurrently overcoming the burden of overthinking. The journey unfolds as a testament to the indomitable human spirit's capacity to reclaim agency, cultivate resilience, and forge a path toward healing and freedom.

1

Understanding Abuse

In the haunting corridors of an abusive relationship, where shadows linger and echoes of pain reverberate, the first step towards liberation is to unravel the intricate layers of abuse that ensnare the spirit. This chapter embarks on a profound exploration, a journey into the heart of darkness where manipulation, control, and anguish converge.

The Spectrum of Abuse

Abuse, a malevolent force, manifests in various forms, leaving scars that extend far beyond the physical realm. As we navigate through the labyrinth of torment, it becomes crucial to decipher the nuanced shades of abuse. Physical violence, with its visible bruises, is the overt expression of malevolence, but the insidious nature of emotional abuse leaves wounds that linger beneath the surface.

Emotional abuse, often the silent assassin, thrives on undermining self-worth through degradation, manipulation, and the relentless erosion of confidence. The scars it leaves may be invisible, but their impact is profound, weaving a tapestry of self-doubt that imprisons the spirit.

Financial abuse, a subtler yet potent form, tightens its grip by controlling economic resources. The manipulation of finances becomes a tool of coercion, trapping victims in a cycle of dependence that further entrenches their vulnerability.

The Cycle of Control

Abusers deploy a repertoire of tactics to maintain dominance, perpetuating a cycle of control that keeps victims ensnared. Gaslighting, a psychological weapon, distorts reality and sows seeds of doubt, leaving victims questioning their own sanity. Isolation becomes another potent tool, cutting off avenues of support and magnifying the abuser's influence.

Understanding the intricacies of this cycle is pivotal. From the tension-building phase to the explosive release of violence, and finally, the remorseful reconciliation—each phase is a thread in the fabric of abuse. By unraveling this cycle, survivors can gain clarity and reclaim agency over their lives.

Signs and Patterns

Recognizing the signs and patterns of abuse is an empowering act. This chapter delves into the behavioral red flags, the subtle cues that betray an abuser's true nature. Through insightful narratives and real-life examples, we bring these patterns into sharp focus, providing a roadmap for those navigating the treacherous terrain of an abusive relationship.

The Psychological Impact

The trauma inflicted by abuse extends beyond the visible wounds, delving deep into the recesses of the psyche. Understanding the profound psychological impact is crucial for both survivors and those aiming to support them. This chapter explores the emotional toll, shedding light on the post-traumatic stress, anxiety, and depression that often accompany the aftermath of abuse.

As we embark on this journey of understanding, let it be a beacon of enlightenment. For only in the illumination of truth can we find the strength to confront abuse head-on and take the first courageous steps towards breaking free from the chains that bind the spirit.

2

Root Causes of Overthinking

I n the labyrinth of an abusive relationship, where the echoes of pain resonate, overthinking emerges as an insidious companion, weaving its threads into the complex tapestry of psychological distress. This chapter plunges into the depths of overthinking, peeling back layers to unveil its roots and exploring the intricate interplay between abuse and the mental turmoil it begets.

Fear and Anxiety

At the core of overthinking lies the visceral response to fear and anxiety—emotions heightened within the crucible of an abusive relationship. The constant threat of unpredictable outbursts and manipulative tactics by an abusive partner breeds an environment where fear thrives. This heightened state of alertness, a survival mechanism, becomes a fertile ground for overthinking, as the mind tirelessly churns through scenarios in an attempt to anticipate and navigate the next potential threat.

Anxiety, the silent accomplice, weaves its tendrils into every facet of daily life. The perpetual uncertainty and unpredictability of living with an abusive partner create a pervasive sense of unease. The mind, grappling with the weight of impending danger, succumbs to a relentless cycle of overthinking—a futile attempt to gain control over the uncontrollable.

Low Self-Esteem

Overthinking and low self-esteem share a symbiotic relationship, each exacerbating the other in the context of an abusive relationship. The constant barrage of criticism, belittlement, and devaluation from an abusive partner corrodes the victim's sense of self-worth. Over time, the insidious whispers of self-doubt become a cacophony, drowning out any semblance of confidence.

As self-esteem dwindles, the mind compensates by over analyzing every action, word, and decision. The relentless quest for approval and validation becomes a driving force behind the ceaseless mental chatter. Overthinking, in this context, becomes a coping mechanism—an attempt to navigate a reality where one's intrinsic value has been systematically eroded.

Learned Helplessness

In the crucible of abuse, victims often find themselves trapped in a cycle of learned helplessness—a psychological state where one believes they have no control over their circumstances. This sense of powerlessness is a fertile breeding ground for overthinking. The mind, devoid of agency, seeks solace in the futile task of dissecting past events, attempting to find a semblance of control in an environment dominated by chaos.

Learned helplessness perpetuates overthinking as victims grapple with the belief that they are powerless to change their situation. The mental treadmill of replaying events, contemplating hypothetical scenarios, and second-guessing decisions becomes an intricate dance with the illusion of control—an illusion that, tragically, remains elusive.

As we navigate the treacherous waters of overthinking within the context of an abusive relationship, understanding these root causes is paramount. It lays the foundation for dismantling the shackles that bind the mind, paving the way for resilience, healing, and ultimately, breaking free from the pervasive grip of overthinking.

3

Breaking the Cycle

Breaking free from the suffocating cycle of overthinking requires an unwavering resilience that goes beyond the surface. It is a transformative act rooted in the strength to face the harsh realities of an abusive relationship and the commitment to navigate the challenging path towards liberation. Resilience, in this context, becomes a powerful force that propels individuals to withstand the psychological pressures inflicted by the abuser and initiate the process of reclaiming control over their own thoughts and emotions.

The metaphorical chains of overthinking are dismantled through a multi-faceted approach. By recognizing and challenging distorted thought patterns, individuals begin to unravel the web of overthinking. Concrete exercises and affirmations are employed to disrupt the negative loops that perpetuate self-doubt and anxiety. The emphasis is on fostering a mindset that promotes self-compassion, self-love, and a belief in one's inherent worth.

Establishing Boundaries

The first crucial step in breaking the cycle of overthinking within the context of an abusive relationship is the establishment of firm and non-negotiable boundaries. These boundaries serve as a fortress, delineating the limits of what is acceptable and unacceptable. By clearly defining personal boundaries, individuals begin to reclaim a sense of autonomy and self-control.

Establishing boundaries is not only a declaration of self-respect but also a powerful deterrent against the incessant mental chatter fueled by over-thinking. As individuals learn to honor their limits, the internal dialogue shifts from self-doubt to self-assertion. This process lays the groundwork for dismantling the cycle of overthinking, providing a sturdy foundation upon which further strategies for liberation can be built.

Building Self-Esteem

A cornerstone in breaking the cycle of overthinking is the deliberate cultivation of self-esteem. The insidious erosion of self-worth perpetuated by an abusive partner requires a conscious effort to rebuild the shattered fragments of one's identity. This chapter delves into empowering exercises and affirmations designed to bolster self-esteem, nurturing the seed of self-worth that has been trampled upon.

As individuals embark on the journey of self-discovery, they confront the distorted narratives that fueled overthinking. By recognizing and challenging these negative thought patterns, a transformative shift occurs—a shift from the victim mentality imposed by abuse to a resilient mindset rooted in self-love and self-empowerment.

Seeking Support from Friends and Family

Breaking the cycle of overthinking is not a solitary endeavor. This chapter explores the importance of seeking support from a network of friends and family. The isolation imposed by an abusive partner is dismantled as individuals reconnect with their support system. The empathetic understanding and encouragement provided by loved ones become a balm for the wounded spirit, counteracting the corrosive effects of overthinking.

Sharing experiences with trusted confidantes not only validates the reality of the abuse but also serves as a reality check for distorted perceptions perpetuated by overthinking. The collective strength of a supportive network becomes a formidable force in breaking the cycle, offering a lifeline to those navigating the tumultuous waters of an abusive relationship.

Breaking the cycle of overthinking is a journey laden with challenges, yet it is a journey toward liberation. As individuals reclaim agency over their thoughts and actions, the cycle of overthinking begins to unravel, paving the way for a renewed sense of self and the promise of a brighter, liberated future.

4

Cognitive Behavioral Techniques

In an abusive relationship, where the mind is often a battleground of torment, cognitive behavioral techniques emerge as powerful tools for individuals seeking liberation from the suffocating grip of overthinking. This chapter delves into the intricacies of these techniques, offering a comprehensive exploration of how they can be harnessed to reframed thoughts, navigate emotional turmoil, and foster a path towards healing.

Identifying and Challenging Negative Thoughts:

Cognitive behavioral techniques begin by shining a light on the negative thought patterns that underpin overthinking. This chapter guides individuals through the process of self-reflection, helping them identify distorted thoughts perpetuated by an abusive partner. By dissecting and challenging these negative cognitions, individuals gain insight into the roots of their overthinking, gradually dismantling the foundations of self-doubt and anxiety.

Concrete exercises, such as keeping a thought journal or engaging in cognitive restructuring, become invaluable tools in this process. Through systematic exploration, individuals learn to question the validity of their negative thoughts, replacing them with more balanced and realistic perspectives. This transformative practice initiates a shift in the cognitive landscape, breaking the cycle of overthinking and fostering a newfound mental resilience.

Mindfulness Practices:

Embedded within the fabric of cognitive behavioral techniques is the profound practice of mindfulness. This chapter explores how cultivating present-moment awareness can serve as a sanctuary from the incessant rumination that characterizes overthinking. Mindfulness techniques, ranging from deep breathing exercises to guided meditation, become anchors in the storm, allowing individuals to detach from the overwhelming thoughts associated with an abusive relationship.

By immersing themselves in the present, individuals gain a reprieve from the burdens of the past and the anxieties about the future. Mindfulness becomes a refuge, providing clarity and a renewed sense of control over one's internal world. This intentional focus on the present moment not only alleviates the mental strain of overthinking but also empowers individuals to respond to challenges with greater resilience.

Reframing Perspectives:

Another pivotal aspect of cognitive behavioral techniques is the art of reframing perspectives. This chapter elucidates how individuals can reshape their interpretations of events, reclaiming agency over the narrative of their lives. By reframing negative experiences, individuals challenge the automatic associations that fuel overthinking and cultivate a mindset of empowerment.

Practical exercises, such as the "ABCDE" technique (Activating Event, Beliefs, Consequences, Disputation, and New Effect), become instrumental in this process. Through deliberate examination and restructuring of thought patterns, individuals gain the ability to view their experiences in a more balanced light. This reframing not only diminishes the power of overthinking but also fosters a sense of control over one's emotional responses.

In essence, the cognitive behavioral techniques explored in this chapter provide a roadmap for individuals seeking relief from the overthinking that often accompanies an abusive relationship. By identifying and challenging negative thoughts, embracing mindfulness practices, and reframing perspectives, individuals embark on a transformative journey. This journey not only breaks the cycle of overthinking but also empowers them to navigate the complexities of an abusive relationship with newfound mental strength and resilience.

5

Legal and safety consideration

In the process of liberating oneself from the burdensome chains of overthinking within an abusive relationship, a crucial focal point emerges which is the imperative understanding of legal and safety considerations. This chapter stands as an exhaustive guide, elucidating the pathways for securing legal protection, formulating effective safety plans, and skillfully navigating the complex landscape essential for safeguarding one's well-being.

Understanding Legal Rights:

In the critical pursuit of liberation from the confines of an abusive relationship, a foundational step begins with a comprehensive understanding of legal rights. Emotional abuse, with its insidious impact on mental well-being, is unveiled, highlighting the significance of recognizing and addressing this often invisible yet deeply harmful aspect. Additionally, the financial dimensions of abuse are explored, acknowledging the manipulation and control exerted by abusers over economic resources.

Through this exploration, individuals gain not only awareness but also a language to articulate their experiences within the legal framework. Recognizing abuse in its multifaceted forms becomes a potent tool for individuals to validate their experiences and seek appropriate legal remedies.

Navigating Divorce And Child Custody

This legal proceedings are often significant factors in the decision to break free from an abusive relationship. As an individual navigating through divorce and child custody, these are things to be put into consideration:

1. Secure Your Safety:
   Prioritize your safety and that of your children throughout the divorce process. If necessary, seek a restraining or protection order to ensure immediate protection from the abusive partner. Communicate with law enforcement, shelters, or support services to create a safety net for yourself and your children.

2. Consult with Professionals:
   Engage with professionals who specialize in domestic abuse cases, including attorneys, therapists, and counselors. Their expertise can be invaluable in guiding you through the legal intricacies and providing emotional support. Seek out professionals who understand the complexities of abuse and can advocate effectively on your behalf.

3. Document Instances of Abuse:
   Maintain meticulous documentation of instances of abuse, including dates, times, and descriptions of incidents. This evidence can be crucial in legal proceedings. Preserve any relevant communication, such as threatening messages or emails, and gather witness statements if possible.

4. Develop a Safety Plan for Custody Exchanges:
   Create a detailed safety plan for child custody exchanges to minimize potential contact with the abusive partner. Choose safe and neutral locations, preferably with security measures in place. Coordinate exchanges through a trusted third party if needed, such as a relative or a professional visitation center.

5. Be Informed About Legal Rights:

Educate yourself about your legal rights concerning divorce and child custody. Understand the specific laws in your jurisdiction, especially those related to domestic abuse. Consult with your attorney to ensure a comprehensive understanding of how the law applies to your unique situation.

6. Seek Supervised Visitation if Necessary:

If there are concerns about the safety of your children during visitation with the abusive partner, consider seeking supervised visitation. This arrangement ensures that visits occur in a controlled and safe environment, often overseen by a professional supervisor.

7. Address Financial Independence:

Take steps to secure your financial independence. Discuss with your attorney the possibility of seeking spousal support or alimony, especially if financial control was a form of abuse. Establish a separate bank account, if possible, and gather documentation of joint assets for equitable division.

8. Prioritize Children's Well-being:

When navigating child custody, prioritize the well-being of your children. Clearly communicate their needs and concerns to your attorney and any court-appointed professionals involved in the case. Demonstrate a willingness to facilitate a healthy relationship between the children and the non-abusive parent.

9. Establish a Support System:

Cultivate a robust support system consisting of friends, family, and professionals. Having a strong support network can provide emotional strength and practical assistance as you navigate the complexities of divorce and child custody.

10. Focus on Healing:

Recognize that healing is a crucial aspect of this process. Seek therapy or counseling to address the emotional aftermath of the abusive relationship. Prioritize self-care and engage in activities that promote your well-being.

Remember, each situation is unique, and consulting with professionals who specialize in domestic abuse and family law is essential. They can offer personalized guidance based on the specific details of your case, ensuring that you approach divorce and child custody with a comprehensive and informed strategy.

6

Empowerment And Healing

In the ongoing narrative of "How to Stop Overthinking Over an Abusive Husband," the exploration of empowerment and healing is a pivotal segment dedicated to guiding individuals on the path of reclaiming their sense of self, fostering resilience, and courageously moving forward after enduring abuse.

1. Rebuilding Self-Identity:

Acknowledging the Shattered Pieces:

Initiating the process of rebuilding self-identity requires a courageous acknowledgment of the shattered pieces left behind by an abusive relationship. This section delves into the raw emotions and self-reflection essential for recognizing the distortions inflicted upon one's sense of self. It invites readers to confront the fragments and understand the impact of the abusive dynamic on their identity.

Self-Compassion as the Foundation:

The narrative unfolds the transformative power of self-compassion as a foundational element in rebuilding self-identity. By treating oneself with kindness and understanding, individuals can begin the mending process. This section provides practical steps, exercises, and affirmations that foster a renewed sense of worth and help individuals reclaim control over their personal narrative.

Engaging in Self-Discovery:

Self-discovery becomes a guiding light in the reconstruction journey. This section unfolds the liberating process of reconnecting with one's authentic self, separate from the labels imposed by the abuser. Engaging in activities that evoke genuine joy and passion is explored as a roadmap for rediscovering and embracing personal identity, encouraging readers to embark on a journey of self-exploration.

2. Developing Resilience:

Cultivating Emotional Strength:

The development of resilience takes center stage, becoming a cornerstone in the narrative. This section delves into practical strategies and practices that cultivate emotional strength, empowering individuals to withstand the aftershocks of abuse and overthinking. It explores the role of therapy, support groups, and introspective exercises in fostering resilience as a crucial component of the healing journey.

Setting Boundaries as a Shield:

Boundaries emerge as a powerful shield against the onslaught of overthinking. This section discusses the importance of establishing and maintaining firm boundaries, both in external relationships and within one's internal dialogue. Through clear communication and assertiveness, individuals fortify themselves against the recurrence of abuse, setting the stage for a more empowered and resilient existence.

Celebrating Progress, No Matter How Small:

The narrative emphasizes the significance of celebrating small victories as integral to resilience. By acknowledging and celebrating progress, individuals reinforce their resilience. This section provides insights into creating a positive feedback loop, where each step forward, no matter how modest, becomes a testament to growing strength and resilience, fostering a sense of accomplishment and motivation.

3. Moving Forward After Abuse:

Charting a New Course:

Moving forward after abuse unfolds as a journey of charting a new course. This section guides individuals through the practical aspects of reclaiming independence—financially, emotionally, and mentally. It explores the steps involved in establishing autonomy and creating a life detached from the shadows of abuse, emphasizing the importance of intentional choices and self-directed growth.

Seeking Professional Guidance:

Professional guidance takes a prominent role in this section, underscoring the importance of seeking therapy and counseling to navigate the challenges of moving forward after abuse. It provides insights into the role of professionals in offering support, guidance, and tools for emotional recovery, acknowledging the expertise needed for a comprehensive healing process.

Fostering Hope and Future Growth:

The narrative concludes with a focus on fostering hope and envisioning future growth. This section explores the role of goal-setting, creating a vision for the future, and embracing opportunities for personal and professional development. Moving forward after abuse becomes not just a necessity but a deliberate and empowering choice, highlighting the transformative potential of hope in shaping a brighter future.

In essence, the exploration of empowerment and healing serves as a comprehensive guide, inviting readers on a transformative journey towards rebuilding self-identity, developing resilience, and courageously moving forward after enduring abuse. Through practical insights, exercises, and narratives, this aspect of the book stands as a beacon of hope and empowerment for those seeking liberation from the clutches of overthinking in the aftermath of an abusive relationship.

7

Resources

As we navigate the complex landscape of overcoming overthinking in the context of an abusive relationship, the seventh section of "How to Stop Overthinking Over an Abusive Husband" serves as a comprehensive guide to invaluable resources. This segment explores three key areas that individuals can leverage on their journey to healing and empowerment.

Hotlines and Support Organizations:

Immediate Assistance:

This segment delves into the vital role of hotlines and support organizations in providing immediate assistance to individuals in distress. It outlines national and local helplines that offer a lifeline for those grappling with overthinking and abusive dynamics. Readers will find insights into the services provided, such as crisis intervention, emotional support, and guidance on safety planning.

Connecting with Support Networks:

Beyond emergency hotlines, the narrative explores support organizations that specialize in assisting survivors of abuse. It emphasizes the importance of connecting with local and online communities, where individuals can share experiences, gain support, and access valuable resources. This segment aims to empower readers with the knowledge of available networks that can become pillars of strength during challenging times.

Therapy and Counseling Options:

Professional Guidance:

The section navigates through the realm of therapy and counseling as essential tools for healing. It provides an in-depth exploration of different therapeutic modalities, including cognitive-behavioral therapy (CBT), trauma-focused therapy, and support groups. By demystifying these options, readers gain insights into the benefits of seeking professional guidance to address the psychological aftermath of overthinking and abuse.

Choosing the Right Therapist:

Practical advice is offered on selecting the right therapist, considering factors such as specialization in trauma and abuse, cultural sensitivity, and personal compatibility. The narrative underscores the importance of recognizing therapy as a collaborative process and encourages individuals to actively participate in their healing journey.

Self-Help Books and Additional Reading:

Empowering Through Knowledge:

This segment introduces readers to a curated list of self-help books and additional reading materials tailored to the complexities of overthinking and abusive relationships. It emphasizes the empowering nature of knowledge and how understanding the dynamics of abuse and recovery can be a catalyst for personal transformation.

Building a Personal Library:

The narrative encourages readers to build a personal library that includes not only self-help books but also memoirs and narratives from survivors who have successfully navigated similar challenges. By providing a comprehensive reading list, this section equips individuals with resources to deepen their understanding and gain insights from diverse perspectives.

By exploring hotlines and support organizations, therapy and counseling options, and a curated list of self-help books, readers are empowered to proactively seek the resources that resonate with their unique journey. This segment acts as a beacon, illuminating the path toward recovery and offering practical tools to break free from the suffocating cycle of overthinking within an abusive relationship.

8

Personal Narratives Of Overcoming Overthinking

Emily's Path to Healing After Emotional Abuse

In this chapter of "How to Stop Overthinking Over an Abusive Husband," we delve into Emily's and Jasmine's poignant narrative—a testament to resilience, vulnerability, and the transformative journey of overcoming overthinking in the aftermath of emotional abuse.

Introduction to Emily's Struggle:

Emily's story unfolds within the shadows cast by emotional abuse, where overthinking became an uninvited companion, whispering doubts and insecurities. The emotional toll was profound, as the scars of manipulation and control left Emily navigating the labyrinth of self-doubt. The persistent overthinking that accompanied the abuse became a constant, haunting presence.

The Emotional Toll:

Emily bravely shares the emotional toll of living in the aftermath of emotional abuse. The narrative paints a vivid picture of the internal struggles, the sleepless nights filled with intrusive thoughts, and the erosion of self-worth. The scars left by the abuser manifested not just on the surface but penetrated deep into the core of Emily's being.

Turning Points in Seeking Help:

The narrative takes a pivotal turn as Emily reaches critical turning points. The decision to seek help becomes a beacon of hope. Emily's journey unfolds through therapy sessions, support groups, and reaching out to trusted allies. These turning points highlight the resilience found within vulnerability—the courage to acknowledge the need for assistance and the strength to take those first steps towards healing.

The Gradual Process of Reclaiming Autonomy:

As Emily's narrative progresses, we witness the gradual process of reclaiming autonomy. Each step forward is a triumph—a declaration of independence from the shackles of overthinking and emotional abuse. The narrative beautifully illustrates moments of self-discovery, as Emily rediscovers personal strengths buried beneath layers of self-doubt.

Strength Found Within Vulnerability:

Emily's story becomes a testament to the strength found within vulnerability. By sharing the raw and unfiltered emotional journey, Emily demonstrates that reaching out for support is not a sign of weakness but a courageous act of self-preservation. Vulnerability becomes the cornerstone of healing, allowing Emily to confront and dismantle the patterns of overthinking that once held sway.

Importance of Seeking Support:

The narrative emphasizes the crucial role of seeking support in the healing process. Emily's journey becomes a compelling example of the transformative power of opening up, whether to friends, family, or professional counselors. The support received becomes a lifeline, guiding Emily through the labyrinth of overthinking towards a place of empowerment and recovery.

Jasmine's Triumph Over Gaslighting

In the collection of personal narratives, Jasmine's story stands out as a powerful exploration of triumph over gaslighting within the confines of an abusive relationship. Her journey becomes a beacon of strength, shedding light on the insidious nature of gaslighting, its profound impact on mental health, and the unwavering steps taken towards breaking free.

Introduction to Jasmine's Struggle:

Jasmine's narrative unfurls within the sinister grip of gaslighting—an emotional manipulation tactic that distorts reality. The gaslighter's web entangles her thoughts, creating a maze of confusion and self-doubt. Jasmine bravely shares the nuances of this struggle, where the lines between reality and distortion blur, and the very essence of her identity is challenged.

The Insidious Nature of Gaslighting:

Jasmine delves into the insidious nature of gaslighting, exposing the deliberate attempts to erode her perception of reality. Each incident becomes a thread in the web of manipulation, weaving doubt into her thoughts. Gaslighting, she articulates, is not just a distortion of facts but a calculated assault on one's sense of self and truth.

Impact on Mental Health:

The toll on Jasmine's mental health becomes a poignant aspect of her narrative. Gaslighting, she reveals, seeped into every facet of her life, leaving emotional scars that extended far beyond the surface. The constant questioning of her own sanity, the erosion of self-esteem, and the isolation induced by gaslighting are vividly portrayed, offering readers a visceral understanding of the psychological devastation wrought by this form of abuse.

Steps Taken Towards Breaking Free:

Jasmine's story takes a courageous turn as she recounts the steps taken towards breaking free from the suffocating grip of gaslighting. The decision to seek therapy and the gradual recognition of the manipulative tactics employed become pivotal moments in her journey. Readers witness the evolution of Jasmine's resilience as she dismantles the distorted reality imposed upon her.

A Source of Inspiration:

Jasmine's triumph becomes a source of inspiration for those grappling with the distortion of reality in abusive dynamics. Through her resilience, she demonstrates that reclaiming one's truth is not just an act of courage but a necessity for mental and emotional well-being. Jasmine's journey invites others to confront the gaslighting shadows and embark on their paths towards healing and liberation.

9

Fidelia's Journey to Liberation

Background

Fidelia found herself entangled in a toxic relationship marked by emotional abuse and relentless overthinking. The constant questioning of her worth and the erosion of her sense of self prompted her to embark on a journey of self-discovery and empowerment.

Establishing Emotional Boundaries:

Recognizing the emotional toll of the relationship, Fidelia took the courageous step of establishing clear emotional boundaries. She communicated assertively with her partner, expressing the need for respect and emotional support. By refusing to internalize hurtful comments and setting limits on disrespectful behavior, Fidelia reclaimed agency over her emotional well-being.

Communicating Non-Negotiables:

One key aspect of Fidelia's strategy was the explicit communication of non-negotiable boundaries. She articulated the behaviors that were unacceptable and made it clear that crossing these boundaries would have consequences. This proactive approach shifted the power dynamic in the relationship, emphasizing that Fidelia was taking control of her own standards for respectful and healthy interactions.

Setting Physical and Digital Boundaries:

Understanding the importance of personal space, Fidelia established physical boundaries to ensure her safety and emotional comfort. This included delineating areas of the home as private and off-limits to her partner. Additionally, she implemented digital boundaries by managing communication channels and limiting access to personal information, creating a sense of autonomy and security.

Seeking Support:

Fidelia's journey also involved seeking support from friends, family, and a therapist. Through open communication with her support network, she fortified her boundaries with external validation and guidance. This network played a crucial role in reinforcing Fidelia's commitment to taking control of her life and breaking free from the overthinking patterns ingrained by the abusive relationship.

Maintaining Consistency:

A key element in Fidelia's success was the consistency in upholding her boundaries. This required resilience and determination, especially when faced with attempts to manipulate or undermine her resolve. By maintaining unwavering consistency, Fidelia sent a clear message that her boundaries were non-negotiable, contributing significantly to the dismantling of the abusive cycle.

Results:

Through the strategic establishment of boundaries, Fidelia experienced a profound transformation. The cycle of overthinking gradually subsided as she regained control over her emotions and decisions. The once suffocating relationship began to lose its grip, and Fidelia emerged stronger, empowered, and equipped with a newfound sense of self.

Key Takeaways for Readers:

1. Identify Your Boundaries:
   Take time to reflect on what boundaries are crucial for your emotional and physical well-being.

2. Communicate Clearly:
   Articulate your boundaries explicitly and communicate them assertively with your partner.

3. Seek Support:
   Build a support network to provide guidance, validation, and encouragement in maintaining your boundaries.

4. Consistency is Key:
   Uphold your boundaries consistently, even in the face of challenges. This unwavering commitment is instrumental in regaining control.

5. Celebrate Progress:
   Acknowledge and celebrate each success in maintaining your boundaries. This positive reinforcement fuels the journey to empowerment.

10

Anita's Journey To Self Re-discovery

The insistent overthinking, like a relentless tempest, was fueled by the toxic dynamics woven into every fiber of Anita's relationship. It cast shadows so profound that they obscured the light from every aspect of her life. In the labyrinth of manipulation and self-questioning, each thought became entangled, creating a web that seemed impossible to unravel. Anita vividly recounts moments of despair when the weight of overthinking threatened to suffocate her, leaving her gasping for the air of clarity and self-assurance.

Yet, Anita's journey takes an empowering turn as she confronts the abyss of overthinking. The catalyst for change emerges as a pivotal revelation—a recognition of the toll on her mental health. Summoning immense courage, she confronts the intricate patterns of abuse that had held her captive. This turning point marks the genesis of her resilience, the birth of a newfound strength as Anita envisions a life unshackled from the suffocating grip of overthinking.

As Anita navigates the tumultuous waters of her relationship, the narrative unfolds the delicate process of self-discovery. Through introspection and the embrace of external support, she unearths her authentic self buried beneath layers of manipulation. This phase of the journey is marked by revelations, each revelation a brushstroke revealing Anita's strengths, values, and the inherent worth obscured by the oppressive dynamics of abuse.

The heart of Anita's story beats with empowering moments that punctuate her odyssey. These instances of courage, whether small victories or monumental strides, stand as testaments to Anita's resilience in the face of adversity. The rhythm of her journey sees her reclaiming autonomy, setting firm boundaries that serve as shields against the arrows of overthinking. Gradually, like a phoenix rising from the ashes, Anita breaks free from the suffocating cycle.

Each empowering moment becomes a beacon of light, illuminating the path toward self-liberation. The courage to say "no," the strength to seek help, and the determination to redefine her narrative—all coalesce into a triumphant symphony that guides Anita toward a newfound sense of agency. Her journey becomes a powerful illustration that breaking free from overthinking is not a linear path but an intricate dance—a dance toward self-rediscovery, towards embracing one's worth and forging a new narrative.

The crux of Anita's narrative lies in the transformative power of resilience—a testament to the indomitable human spirit. Fueled by self-discovery and courage, resilience becomes the beacon that leads Anita to liberation. Her journey serves as an anthem, underscoring the truth that breaking free from overthinking in an abusive relationship is not just an act of courage but a dance—a courageous dance towards self-rediscovery and the reclamation of a life unburdened by the shadows of abuse.

Conclusion

In concluding "How to Stop Overthinking Over an Abusive Husband," let's revisit the core strategies explored throughout this book. We've delved into understanding abuse dynamics, unraveling the roots of overthinking, and applying cognitive behavioral techniques. Legal considerations, crafting safety plans, and seeking professional help have been highlighted as crucial aspects of reclaiming autonomy. The journey involves not just breaking free from the chains but also rebuilding a life anchored in resilience and self-discovery.

To the readers who have embarked on this journey, your strength is immeasurable. Breaking free from overthinking in an abusive relationship is a courageous endeavor, and your commitment to change is commendable. In the face of adversity, remember that seeking help is not a sign of weakness but a powerful act of self-love. You are not alone; a community of support surrounds you. Take each step forward with the understanding that every stride contributes to your liberation.

The heart of this book lies in the acknowledgment that healing is not an endpoint but a continuous journey. As you navigate the complexities of abuse, overthinking, and recovery, remember that your journey is uniquely yours. Embrace the process of rebuilding self-identity, developing resilience, and moving forward after abuse. The transformative power of resilience and the indomitable human spirit are your allies. Each small victory is a triumph, and every moment of self-discovery is a step towards reclaiming your life.

In closing, breaking free from overthinking in an abusive relationship is not just a destination—it is a courageous dance towards self-rediscovery, empowerment, and recovery. May this book serve as a guide, offering insights and encouragement on your path towards healing. The journey is challenging, but you are stronger than you know. May the chapters of your life ahead be filled with the empowering narratives of resilience, self-love, and the triumph of the human spirit.